RESCUING Animals FROM DISASTERS

SAVING ANIMALS FROM
HURRICANES

by Stephen Person

Consultants: Charlotte Bass Lilly, CEO and President
Animal Rescue New Orleans (ARNO)

Caren Carney, D.V.M.

BEARPORT
PUBLISHING

New York, New York

Credits

Cover and Title Page, © TK; 4, © Travis Heying/KRT/Newscom; 5, © Norman Ng/KRT/Newscom; 6, © G. Fabiano/Sipa Press/Newscom; 7, © Lee Celano/Reuters/Landov; 9, © Science Faction/SuperStock; 10, © Louis DeLuca/Dallas Morning News/Corbis; 11T, © Jerry Grayson/Helifilms Australia PTY Ltd/Getty Images; 11B, © Jason Reed/Reuters/Landov; 12, © Troy Snow/Best Friends Animal Society; 13, © Carlos Barria/Reuters/Landov; 14, © Janice Tuma/Dire Straits Companion Animal Rescue; 15, © AP Photo/Mark Gilliland; 16, © David R. Frazier Photolibrary, Inc./Alamy; 17, © AP Photo/Rogelio Solis; 18, © Robin May/ZUMA Press/Newscom; 19, © Carol Guzy/The Washington Post/Getty Images; 20, © Mario Tama/Getty Images; 21L, © Audubon Nature Institute, New Orleans; 21R, © AP Photo/Cheryl Gerber; 22, © Tier und Naturfotografie/SuperStock; 23, Courtesy of Duke University; 24, Courtesy of NOAA; 25, © AP Photo/Steve Helber; 26, © Robin May/ZUMA Press/Newscom; 27, © Janice Tuma/Dire Straits Companion Animal Rescue; 28, © TK; 29, © AP Photo/ Texas Parks & Wildlife Dept.; 31, © Gregory Pelt/Shutterstock; 32, © Caitlin Mirra/Shutterstock.

Publisher: Kenn Goin
Editorial Director: Adam Siegel
Creative Director: Spencer Brinker
Design: Dawn Beard Creative and Kim Jones
Photo Researcher: Picture Perfect Professionals, LLC

Library of Congress Cataloging-in-Publication Data

Person, Stephen.
  Saving animals from hurricanes / by Stephen Person.
      p. cm. — (Rescuing animals from disasters)
  Includes bibliographical references and index.
  ISBN-13: 978-1-61772-290-5 (library binding)
  ISBN-10: 1-61772-290-1 (library binding)
  1. Animal rescue—Juvenile literature. 2. Hurricanes—Juvenile literature. I. Title.
  QL83.2.P478 2012
  636.08'32—dc22
                                    2011007783

For more information, write to Bearport Publishing Company, Inc., 45 West 21st Street, Suite 3B, New York, New York 10010. Printed in the United States of America in North Mankato, Minnesota.

070111
042711CGC

10 9 8 7 6 5 4 3 2 1

CONTENTS

Animals Everywhere

A newspaper reporter named Cathy Scott sat in a small boat. She was not on a river or a lake, though—she was floating down the streets of New Orleans, Louisiana. It was early September 2005, and most of the city was **flooded**. Deep water lapped against the porches of **abandoned** homes. The silent neighborhood seemed to be empty.

Dogs and cats were stuck all over New Orleans with no food or clean water.

In the boat with Cathy were two animal rescuers, Tracey Simmons and Mike Bzdewka. "Watch this," Tracey said. She began barking like a dog. Suddenly, the street seemed to explode with the sounds of animals! From houses all around came dog barks and cat meows. Cathy now realized there were animals everywhere. Unfortunately, they were scared, hungry, and all alone.

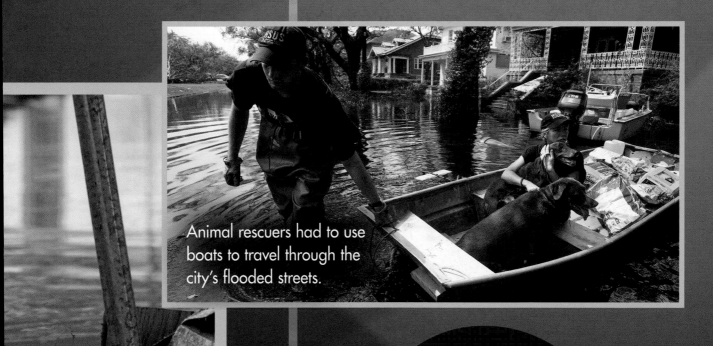

Animal rescuers had to use boats to travel through the city's flooded streets.

Tracey and Mike were working with Best Friends Animal Society, an **animal sanctuary** based in Utah. They were among many people who came to the New Orleans region to help rescue animals.

Dog on a Car Roof

Following the sound of a cat's meow, Mike guided the boat to the porch of a house. He jumped into the waist-high water and splashed his way to the window. He opened it, lifted a cat gently out of the house, and carried her to the boat. Then he turned the boat to the next home, following the sounds of a barking dog. Once they reached the driveway, Mike, Tracey, and Cathy found what they were looking for—a dog sitting on the roof of a car.

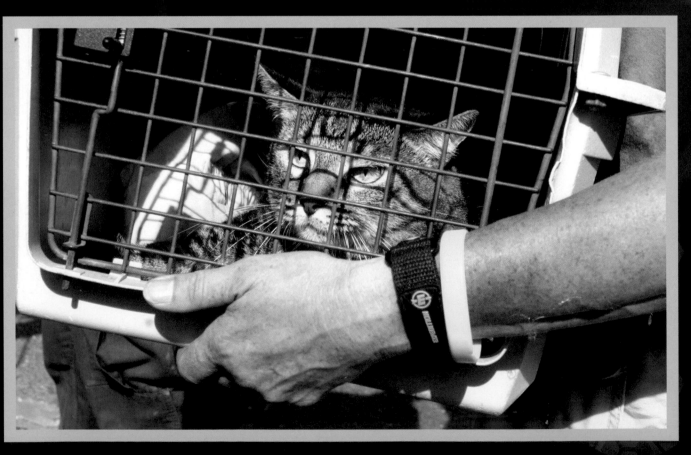

Rescuers came prepared with cages for dogs and cats.

Wearing tall rubber boots, Tracey stepped into the muddy water. As soon as the dog spotted her, he jumped off the car's roof and into the flooded street toward Tracey. She was then able to scoop him up and bring him safely to the boat. The cat and dog sat quietly in the boat as the rescue team moved on to continue their search for other animals that were trapped in the flooded city.

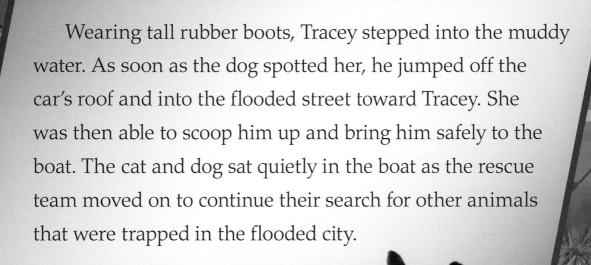

To stay dry, animals found places to rest on the roofs of cars and houses.

People from around the country sent food, money, and medicine to help animals trapped in New Orleans. Groups such as the Humane Society of the United States collected **donations** for the animals.

Hurricane Katrina

Why were so many animals trapped in the city of New Orleans? In August 2005, **Tropical Storm** Katrina formed over the Atlantic Ocean and began moving slowly west. **Meteorologists** watched carefully as the storm gained strength and its winds gained speed. On August 25, Katrina became what many people had feared—a **hurricane**.

Katrina's Path: From Storm to Hurricane

Tropical storms have winds of 39 miles per hour (63 kph) or faster. About half of all tropical storms gain strength over the ocean and become hurricanes, which have winds of 74 miles per hour (119 kph) or faster.

This map shows the path of Katrina as it changed from a tropical storm to a hurricane.

Meteorologists spread the warning that Hurricane Katrina was headed right for the **Gulf Coast** of the United States—and it was coming in just a few days! The mayor of New Orleans ordered everyone to **evacuate** the city. People had to leave quickly, and many were not able to take their pets. Instead, they left extra food and water for the animals—thinking they would be back in just a few days.

Hurricane Katrina forced more than 800,000 people in Louisiana, Mississippi, and Alabama to leave their homes.

Pets Left Behind

On August 29, 2005, Hurricane Katrina slammed the Gulf Coast with heavy rain and winds that whipped at speeds of up to 140 miles per hour (225 kph). The ferocious winds caused a huge wall of water called a **storm surge** to race from the Gulf toward land. It crashed into New Orleans's **levees**, wall-like structures that were built to protect the city from flooding.

Hurricane Katrina destroyed buildings all along the coast of Louisiana, Mississippi, and Alabama. This photo shows damage in Gulfport, Mississippi.

The storm surge was so powerful that the levees around New Orleans **collapsed**. Water began pouring into the city. Government rescuers raced to save people who were still stuck in New Orleans. Unfortunately, they had no time to save the animals that lived there. As a result, hundreds of thousands of pets were stuck in the flooded city.

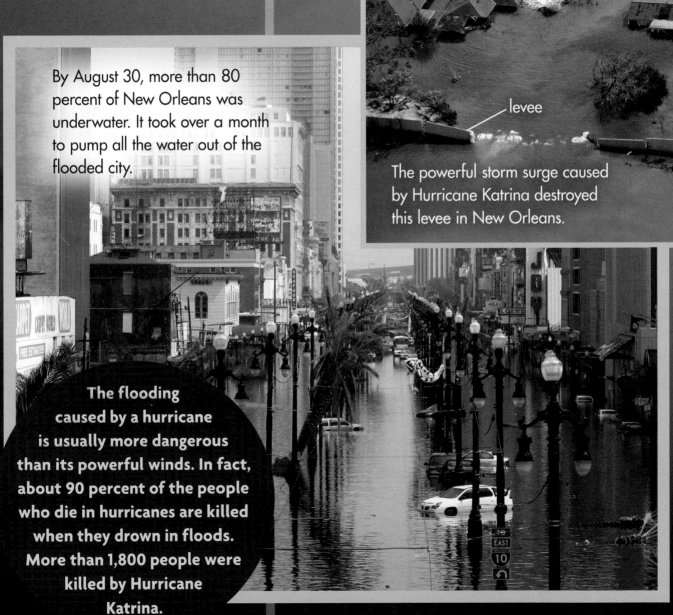

By August 30, more than 80 percent of New Orleans was underwater. It took over a month to pump all the water out of the flooded city.

levee

The powerful storm surge caused by Hurricane Katrina destroyed this levee in New Orleans.

The flooding caused by a hurricane is usually more dangerous than its powerful winds. In fact, about 90 percent of the people who die in hurricanes are killed when they drown in floods. More than 1,800 people were killed by Hurricane Katrina.

Rescuers Rush In

News of the **stranded** animals spread around the country. One of the many **volunteers** who rushed to New Orleans was Jane Garrison, an animal rescuer from South Carolina. "I could not stop thinking about these animals trapped in homes," Jane said.

Pictures like this one appeared on television, in newspapers, and on the Internet. After seeing them, people rushed to New Orleans to help rescue the stranded animals.

Jane spent the next six weeks saving animals. She had to break into ruined houses by smashing open doors or windows. "We searched under beds, in attics and closets," Jane said. She found animals still alive even weeks after the storm. "I rescued a dog off a roof who had been up there for 17 days," she said. "He weighed 40 pounds (18 kg) when he should have weighed 95 (43 kg). He had no access to food, water, or shade—it was 100°F (38°C) there."

Before Katrina, Jane Garrison (left) had rescued animals from many natural disasters, including tornadoes in Arkansas and floods in California.

Jane and other rescuers did not save only dogs and cats. They also rescued birds, turtles, hamsters, lizards, snakes, rabbits, and fish.

Happy Reunions

Rescued animals were carried by boat out of the flooded streets of New Orleans. Volunteers then drove the animals to shelters set up in fairgrounds and schools near the city. A woman named Jan Tuma went to work at a large shelter. Each night, vans drove up with more animals. "Most of us had already worked twelve hours," Jan said. Even though they were tired, Jan and the other volunteers went back to work helping the new arrivals.

Jan Tuma came from her home in Chicago to help rescue animals in New Orleans.

Jan worked with dogs. First she gave them water and food. If the dogs looked sick or **injured**, she then took them to a **veterinarian**. Other volunteers took pictures of the animals and posted them on the Internet. This helped owners find their pets. Jan saw many happy **reunions** between people and pets due to the photos owners had seen on the Internet.

No one knows exactly how many animals were killed because of Hurricane Katrina. It is **estimated** that more than 100,000 pets died in the days and weeks after the hurricane.

This woman from New Orleans found her cat Sweetie at a shelter in Tennessee.

The Horse Hero

Not all the Gulf Coast animals that were in danger were pets. Lucien Mitchell took care of horses and mules that worked for a **carriage** company in New Orleans. Unfortunately, there was not enough time to get all the animals out before Katrina hit. Twenty-two horses and mules were stuck in the stable. Lucien, however, refused to leave without them.

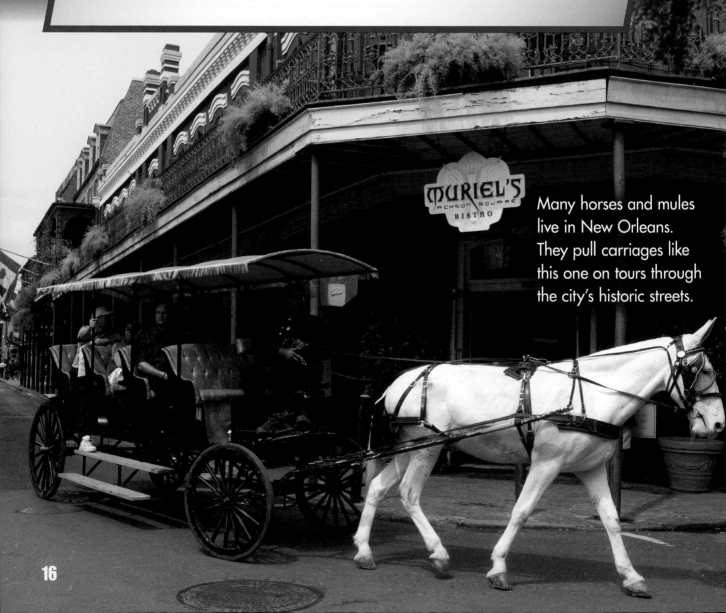

Many horses and mules live in New Orleans. They pull carriages like this one on tours through the city's historic streets.

As the storm raged, water rose above the animals' chests. To save them, Lucien and a coworker pulled the horses and mules through the flooded streets. They were headed toward a park that was on higher ground. To get there, they had to swim next to the animals in some spots. Amazingly, the two men kept the horses and mules alive for nearly a week, until rescuers arrived with trailers to take the animals to safety.

Animals on farms all over the Gulf Coast region were killed because of Hurricane Katrina. Many cows and horses drowned, or were killed when barns collapsed.

Hundreds of thousands of chickens died after being stuck for days in cages without clean drinking water.

Molly's Story

A pony named Molly was another horse that Katrina almost killed. After the hurricane, Molly was left alone in a barn for more than two weeks. When rescuers finally came, they took her to a nearby farm. It seemed as though Molly would finally be safe. However, dogs that had been rescued from the hurricane were also living on the farm. One of them attacked Molly, badly injuring her front right leg.

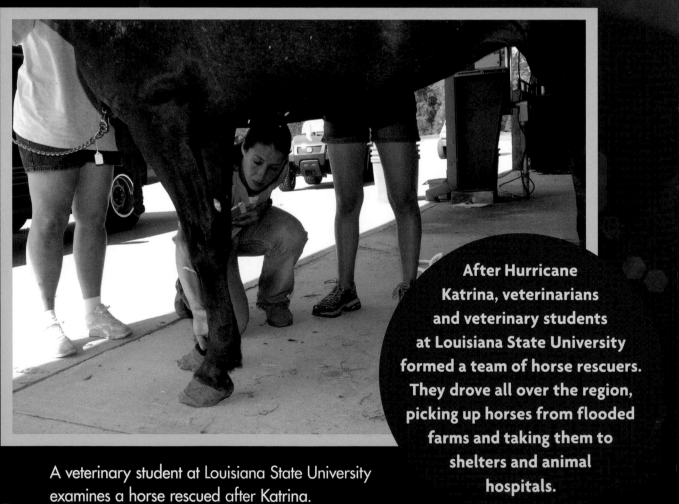

A veterinary student at Louisiana State University examines a horse rescued after Katrina.

After Hurricane Katrina, veterinarians and veterinary students at Louisiana State University formed a team of horse rescuers. They drove all over the region, picking up horses from flooded farms and taking them to shelters and animal hospitals.

When veterinarians from Louisiana State University heard about Molly, they volunteered to help her. They removed the pony's leg below the knee and attached a replacement leg made out of plastic and metal. Molly slowly learned to walk and trot with her new leg. As news of the pony's recovery spread, children who had also lost a leg or an arm began coming to visit Molly. Her strength and courage have helped give many young people hope for the future.

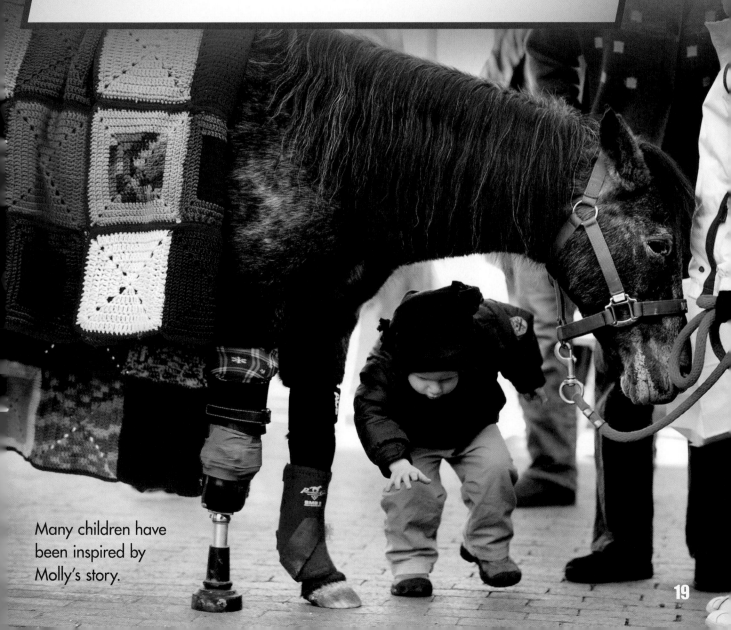

Many children have been inspired by Molly's story.

Police at the Aquarium

Don Kinney, a New Orleans police officer, also became an animal rescuer during Katrina. As the hurricane moved through the city, powerful winds smashed buildings, brought down power lines, and knocked out electricity. This put animals at the Aquarium of the Americas in danger. Why? Electricity is needed to run the machines that clean water tanks and pump in the **oxygen** fish need to breathe. When there was no electricity, nearly 10,000 fish died at the aquarium. Even more animals would have died, however, without Don's quick thinking.

Nineteen penguins went to live at a California aquarium while the Aquarium of the Americas was being repaired. They returned to New Orleans, as shown here, in 2006.

Don found the aquarium refrigerators. He filled buckets with the fish and meat that had been stored there. He then walked around the building with a flashlight, feeding fish to the otters and penguins. He tossed hunks of meat to the alligator. Don spent several days caring for the animals. At night, he slept on a bench in the aquarium. Without his help, many of the animals would have starved to death.

About 2,000 animals at the Aquarium of the Americas, including this white alligator, survived Katrina.

As Hurricane Katrina approached land, the **staff** of the Audubon Zoo in New Orleans had no time to move big animals, like giraffes and elephants, so many of the workers stayed behind to care for them.

"It gave me a good feeling in my heart knowing I was feeding animals and keeping them alive," said New Orleans police officer Don Kinney. This picture shows Don with his pet parrot, Yogi.

Eight Missing Dolphins

An aquarium in Gulfport, Mississippi, was hit even harder than the one in New Orleans. Marine Life Oceanarium was home to many large animals, including sea lions and dolphins. As Katrina moved toward the Mississippi coast, workers put sea lions in crates and moved them farther **inland**. However, eight Atlantic bottlenose dolphins were left in a 30-foot-high (9-m) tank at Marine Life. The staff thought they would be safe there.

In the wild, dolphins such as these can hunt and catch their own food, including fish and squid.

The dolphins at Marine Life Oceanarium had lived in **captivity** for most of their lives. They did not know how to hunt for themselves or protect themselves from **predators**, such as sharks.

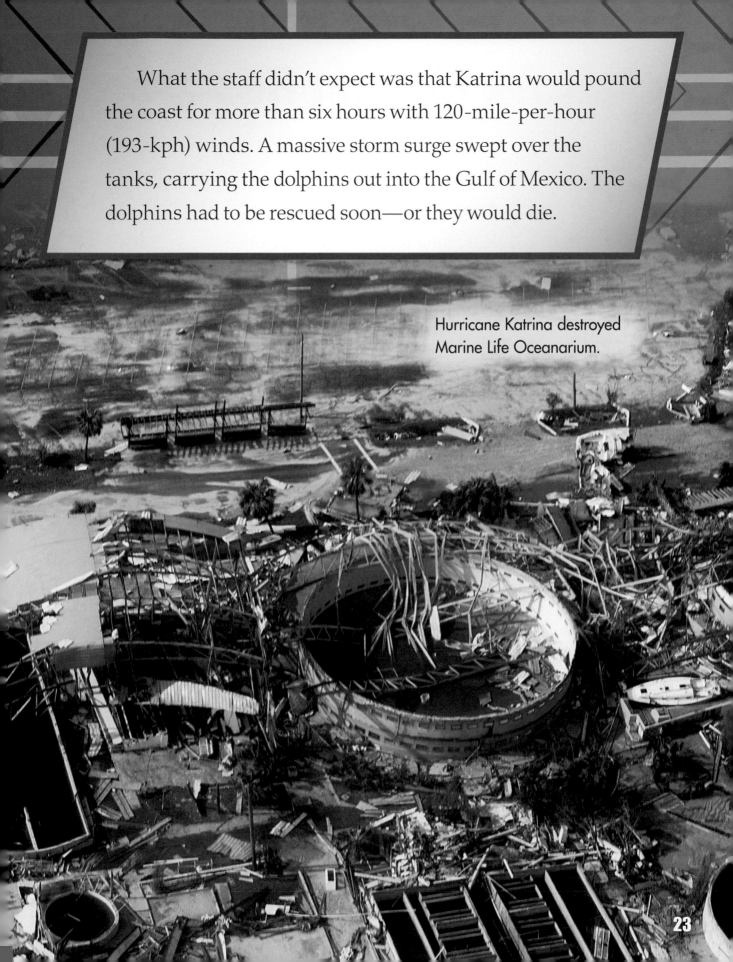

What the staff didn't expect was that Katrina would pound the coast for more than six hours with 120-mile-per-hour (193-kph) winds. A massive storm surge swept over the tanks, carrying the dolphins out into the Gulf of Mexico. The dolphins had to be rescued soon—or they would die.

Hurricane Katrina destroyed Marine Life Oceanarium.

An Ocean Rescue

Twelve days after Katrina struck, Marine Life staff were able to begin looking for the missing dolphins. They used a boat and a helicopter to search the **coastal** waters near Gulfport. In less than 15 minutes, the helicopter crew saw a group of dolphins swimming near shore. The workers in the boat sped toward them. The animals were hungry and weak, and many had injuries from the storm, but the rescuers had found what they were looking for—the missing dolphins!

On September 10, the team of rescuers found the missing dolphins.

To build up the animals' strength, the staff put medicine inside fish and fed them to the dolphins. The next challenge was to figure out how to bring the animals back to shore. To help with this, dolphin trainers went out in boats. They taught the dolphins to jump onto floating mats. The mats were then pulled to land by boat, and the dolphins were placed in swimming pools—safe at last.

Marine Life trainers had to teach the dolphins to jump onto floating mats. Luckily, dolphins are very smart and learned quickly how to do this.

When the dolphins were healthy enough to travel, they were moved to a new home in the Bahamas.

The Biggest Animal Rescue

More than 15,000 animals were rescued after Hurricane Katrina. In fact, this effort was the largest animal rescue in history. Luckily, many of the animals were eventually reunited with their owners. When their owners could not be found, animals were **adopted** by new ones. Jan Tuma was one of the volunteers who returned home with a new pet.

This couple was reunited with their missing puppies at the Lamar-Dixon rescue center in Gonzales, Louisiana. Set up by the Louisiana SPCA (Society for the Prevention of Cruelty to Animals), the center became the largest animal shelter and animal rescue operation in U.S. history.

Jan took home a badly injured dog that had lost one front leg and broken the other. She named the brave dog Hurricane. When she looks at Hurricane, Jan is reminded of a saying she heard often from animal rescuers—"Saving just one dog won't change the world, but it surely will change the world for that one dog."

In 2006, the United States government passed a new law that says during future disasters or emergencies, states must do more to help rescue, care for, and shelter people's pets.

These pictures show Jan's dog Hurricane shortly after being rescued in New Orleans (above) and after recovering for a few months at his new home in Chicago (right).

FAMOUS HURRICANES AND RESCUES

While Hurricane Katrina led to the largest animal rescue in history, other big hurricanes have also put animals in danger.

Hurricane Mitch

- In October 1998, Hurricane Mitch hit several countries in Central America, including Honduras and Nicaragua, killing about 11,000 people. More than 50,000 animals died, and many more were hurt.

- The World Society for the Protection of Animals raced to Central America to help animals in danger.

- Veterinarians traveled through areas hit by the storm, treating horses, cows, and other animals.

- Volunteers worked with local governments to move animals away from flooded areas to higher ground. The animals were given food and a safe place to live.

Hurricane Ike

- In September 2008, meteorologists warned that a massive storm called Hurricane Ike was moving toward the coast of Texas. People began to evacuate coastal areas. Many animals were left behind.

- The Houston SPCA (Society for the Prevention of Cruelty to Animals) helped lead an animal rescue effort. Before the storm hit, the SPCA evacuated 300 dogs, 400 cats, and 60 horses. The animals were taken to shelters farther inland.

- After the hurricane, volunteers cared for more than 1,000 baby animals whose parents were killed by Ike.

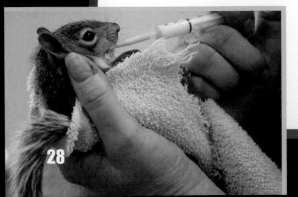

Hurricane Ike knocked hundreds of baby squirrels out of nests in trees. People gathered the squirrels and took them to shelters, where they were fed by volunteers.

ANIMALS AT RISK FROM HURRICANES

Animal rescuers often focus on saving cats, dogs, and other pets. Hurricanes, however, are also dangerous to animals living on farms and in the wild.

Farm Animals

- Hurricanes put farm animals in danger because high winds can knock over barns, and heavy rains can cause flooding.

- When people evacuate farms, animals are sometimes left alone, with no food or clean drinking water.

- During Hurricane Ike, thousands of cows drowned in floods. Others were able to swim to dry areas. Some swam for hours before reaching a place where they could stand.

Cowboys rounded up cattle and drove them to safety after Hurricane Ike hit Texas.

Wildlife

- Hurricanes can kill wildlife and can also cause young animals to become separated from their parents. Without help, most baby animals cannot live long in the wild.

- When Hurricane Dennis hit Florida in 2005, more than 150 baby pelicans were orphaned. Animal rescuers cared for the birds for seven months, until they were strong enough to be released back into their **habitat**.

- When Hurricane Earl hit Nova Scotia, Canada, in 2010, the high winds injured many birds. The winds blew birds into trees and buildings, causing broken bones. Rescuers took the injured birds to shelters and took care of them until they could be released.

GLOSSARY

abandoned (uh-BAN-duhnd) left empty; no longer used

adopted (uh-DOPT-id) taken in as part of a family

animal sanctuary (AN-uh-muhl SANGK-choo-er-ee) a place where homeless animals can stay for the rest of their lives

captivity (kap-TIV-uh-tee) places where animals live in which they are cared for by people and which are not the animals' natural environments

carriage (KA-rij) a vehicle that has wheels, often pulled by horses

coastal (KOHST-uhl) having to do with the area of land that runs along an ocean

collapsed (kuh-LAPST) fell down or caved in

donations (doh-NAY-shuhns) gifts of money or supplies to help people, causes, or organizations in need

estimated (ESS-tuh-mayt-id) to have figured out the approximate amount of something

evacuate (i-VAK-yoo-ayt) to leave a dangerous place or to remove people or animals from a dangerous place

flooded (FLUHD-id) covered with water, often by heavy rains or overflowing rivers

Gulf Coast (GULF KOHST) the area made up of the coasts of Texas, Louisiana, Mississippi, Alabama, and Florida—the states that border the Gulf of Mexico.

habitat (HAB-uh-tat) the place in nature where a plant or animal normally lives

hurricane (HUR-uh-kayn) a storm that forms over the ocean, with heavy rains and winds of at least 74 miles per hour (119 kph)

injured (IN-jurd) hurt

inland (IN-land) on land, away from the water

levees (LEV-eez) high walls made of earth, concrete, or other material built next to a body of water to prevent flooding

meteorologists (mee-tee-ur-OL-uh-jists) scientists who study weather

oxygen (OK-suh-juhn) a colorless gas that is found in the air and water, and that animals and people need to breathe

predators (PRED-uh-turz) animals that hunt other animals for food

reunions (ree-YOON-yuhnz) meetings between animals or people who have not been together for a long time

staff (STAF) people who work for a business or an organization

storm surge (STORM SURJ) a rise in the level of the ocean caused by a hurricane or a tropical storm

stranded (STRAND-id) stuck somewhere without a way to leave

tropical storm (TROP-uh-kuhl STORM) a circular storm that forms over the ocean, with heavy rains and winds of between 39 and 73 miles per hour (63 and 117 kph)

veterinarian (vet-ur-uh-NAIR-ee-uhn) a doctor who cares for animals

volunteers (vol-uhn-TIHRZ) people who offer to do a job without getting paid

BIBLIOGRAPHY

Animal Rescue New Orleans
(www.animalrescueneworleans.org/archive.html)

The Institute for Marine Mammal Studies
(http://imms.org/rescue.php)

PBS Film "Storm That Drowned a City"
(www.pbs.org/wgbh/nova/orleans/)

READ MORE

Aronin, Miriam. *Mangled by a Hurricane! (Disaster Survivors).* New York: Bearport (2010).

Kaster, Pam. *Molly the Pony: A True Story.* Baton Rouge, LA: Louisiana State University Press (2008).

Larson, Kirby, and Mary Nethery. *Two Bobbies: A True Story of Hurricane Katrina, Friendship, and Survival.* New York: Walker Books for Young Readers (2008).

LEARN MORE ONLINE

To learn more about rescuing animals from hurricanes, visit
www.bearportpublishing.com/RescuingAnimalsfromDisasters

INDEX

ABOUT THE AUTHOR

Stephen Person has written many children's books about history, science, and the environment. He lives with his family in Saratoga Springs, New York.